FELTING FOR KIDS

Martingale®
& COMPANY

FELTING
FOR KIDS

Fun Toys,
Cool Accessories

Gry Højgaard Jacobsen and Sif Højgaard Hoverby

Felting for Kids: Fun Toys, Cool Accessories
© 2009 by Gry Højgaard Jacobsen
and Sif Højgaard Hoverby

Martingale & Company
20205 144th Ave. NE
Woodinville, WA 98072-8478 USA
www.martingale-pub.com

Credits

President & CEO: Tom Wierzbicki
Editor in Chief: Mary V. Green
Managing Editor: Tina Cook
Translator: Carol Huebscher Rhoades
Developmental Editor: Karen Costello Soltys
Technical Editor: Nancy Mahoney
Copy Editor: Sheila Chapman Ryan
Design Director: Stan Green
Production Manager: Regina Girard
Supplemental Illustration: Laurel Strand
Cover & Text Designer: Stan Green

Mission Statement

Dedicated to providing quality products and service
to inspire creativity.

Printed in China
14 13 12 11 10 09   8 7 6 5 4 3 2 1

**Library of Congress Cataloging-in-Publication Data
is available upon request.**

ISBN: 978-1-56477-9335

CONTENTS

BABY 14

PRINCESS 48

LOVE 86

COOL 112

FOREWORD

We never dreamt when we were young that wool and felting would become a large part of our lives, but it wasn't by chance that we've devoted ourselves to something creative. We are sisters who grew up in a household where there was always some type of handcraft under way.

We had tried feltmaking in a small way, but didn't seriously latch on to it until a backpacking trip in 2001. We arrived in Nepal at a time when feltmaking was part of the country's handcrafting culture. Eventually an idea was born: we could produce felted figures with a Scandinavian look. We bought a handful of dyes, sketched a few ideas, and hired some locals to make the felt. They were quite amazed since they had never seen a turquoise horse, pink elephants, or spotted teddy bears. There was a lot of giggling but soon we had a few models we could take home in our backpacks.

Back home in Denmark, we showed the models to friends who reacted so positively that we took the bull by the horns and presented them to a few shops. Their reaction was also positive. Now we definitely had the basis for getting production underway.

In 2002, we premiered our company—Én Gry & Sif—at a small product show called Formland in Herning, Denmark. It went well from the start, not just in Denmark but all around Europe and in the U.S. We were soon known as the two fair Danish sisters with the colorful and imaginative felt models.

Six years have passed since we discovered felting in Nepal and now we employ about 500 women there. We are very pleased to work with a Danida project, which offers better conditions for the workers.

Felting is a wonderful hobby, and we called this book *Felting for Kids* partly because the items in the book are suitable for children of all ages and partly

because felting is a great way to explore crafts with children. To work with wool, water, and soap is pure magic, and children as young as kindergartners can help with making simple items such as balls if they get some help with the shaping.

The young models in this book are our children plus our nieces and nephews, and, as the photos on these pages show, we've had a lot of fun and wonderful family moments with our felting.

It is our hope that many people—big and small— will enjoy our book and its felted pieces.

Best wishes,

Gry and Sif

You get really clean fingers when you felt.

Anyone can join in.

It's so exciting—what will it be?

See what I've made.

FELTING

Wool batts

Wool roving

The Process

Have you washed a wool sweater in water that was too warm? If so, then you know what it means to felt! The wool shrinks and becomes tighter and firmer. You've probably also experienced what happens when youngsters have snowball fights outside in the winter. After constant rubbing and contact with the wet snow, wool mittens become very compacted.

In order for wool to felt, two things are necessary—water and agitation. Wool felts because its fibers are covered with scales. When wool is wet, the scales raise and become barb-like. Agitation causes the scales to interlock.

The technique of felting has been around since the beginning of time. Stories tell that when the animals left Noah's ark, they trod over a felt carpet. The wool from the animals was mixed with urine, and then trampled by feet and hooves. When the wool dried, it was transformed into a large felted carpet. We don't know if this legend is true or not, but it's a fun story.

Ready-Made Felt Or...

On the following pages, you'll learn how to felt fabric, but you can also use ready-made felt for some of the projects in this book. On page 127, we list resources for felt. Commercial felt can be used for any of the designs that are sewn rather than felted together.

Materials and Tools

Wool

In order to felt, you need only one simple material—wool.

The wool used for felting comes in batts. It's wool that has been washed, carded, and sometimes dyed. Wool batts can also be used for spinning into yarn but we use them for felting.

There are two types of carded wool. The first type, called tops, has been carded into long strips with parallel fibers. The other type is roving, which has fibers less well arranged. We prefer tops, which are often rolled into large balls.

For felting, you can use either lamb's wool or Australian merino. Merino is especially fine while most lamb's wool is usually a bit coarser than merino. We've used lamb's wool for the projects in this book.

Water and Soap

As we mentioned earlier, wool has to be thoroughly wetted with water to become felt. The process is facilitated with soap, which works as a surfactant in the water.

Pour a quarter cup of soap flakes into a bowl and dissolve them with a quart of lukewarm water. After the wool has been laid out and saturated with water, it's a good idea to have extra soap on hand. A bar of hand soap is useful for soaping up your fingers.

Bubble Wrap

In order for wool to felt completely, it helps to rub it for a period of time. One method is to rub it over a layer of bubble wrap, as shown in the photo on page 12. Bubble wrap is normally used for packaging, but it's also really good for felting. A lot of people work the wool over bamboo mats, but we think bubble wrap works better.

Curtain Material, Plastic Netting, or Organza

When you need to hold loose pieces in place, such as stars, hearts, and other wool embellishments, it helps to lay curtaining, plastic netting, or organza over the loose pieces until they are firmly felted.

While you are felting, it's important that you lift the curtaining, plastic netting, or organza occasionally so that it won't be felted to the wool.

Felting Needles

Smaller pieces, such as letters, can be attached by needle felting. Felting needles have small barbs that push and felt the fibers into the base.

Blanket Stitch and Crocheted Edging

Blanket Stitch

Many of the projects in this book are joined with a hand blanket stitch using wool yarn in a matching color as the "thread." This becomes part of the overall effect since the stitches are very visible.

As shown below, the stitches are hand sewn from left to right along a line. On larger items, it's best to machine sew the pieces together first, with wrong sides together and using a ¼" seam allowance. The stitching line can then be used to align the blanket stitch.

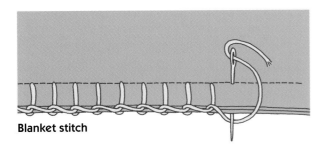

Blanket stitch

Crocheted Edging

Several of the pillows in the book have crocheted edgings. There are two methods for working the crochet. You can crochet the edging separately, and then sew it on, or you can crochet directly onto the pillow backing fabric. (If the felt for your pillow is very thick, it's better to use fabric for the backing rather than more felt.)

Crochet a strip from left to right. Measure the circumference of the pillow and make a single crochet chain long enough to go around the pillow. Turn and chain two. Repeat the following procedure: *one single crochet, skip one chain, four double crochet, skip one chain.*

Crocheted edging

MAKING FELT

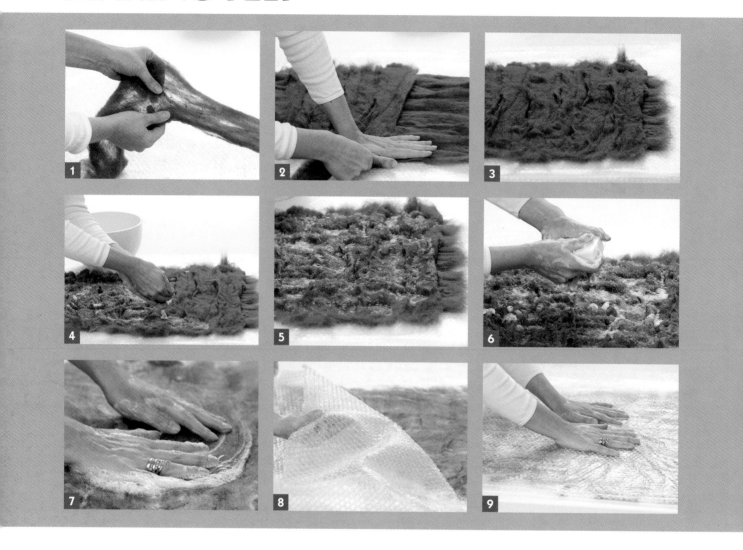

These pages explain how to make a piece of felt. This technique is the starting point for many of the projects in this book. When you are laying out the wool, don't forget that wool can shrink as much as 33% as you felt it. Take that shrinkage into consideration when you measure out the layers of wool at the beginning of the process.

1. Separate the wool a bit so it isn't too compacted.

2–3. Lay the strips of wool side by side over a piece of bubble wrap. The plastic should be at least twice the size of the wool layers. First lay out the wool in one direction, and then make a second layer perpendicular to the first one. Make sure the layers are as even as possible.

4–5. Sprinkle soapy water over the wool until it's saturated. Some people like to use a sprinkling bottle for this but we just sprinkle by hand. It goes more quickly that way.

6. Rub a bar of soap in your hands until your hands are very soapy.

7. Now start the felting process by rubbing the wool with circular hand motions. You have to be patient— you can't be too careful here. It also helps to place a piece of curtaining, plastic netting, or organza over the wool to hold the fibers in place while you felt.

8. When the wool begins to cohere, cover it with bubble wrap.

9. Smooth out the bubble wrap.

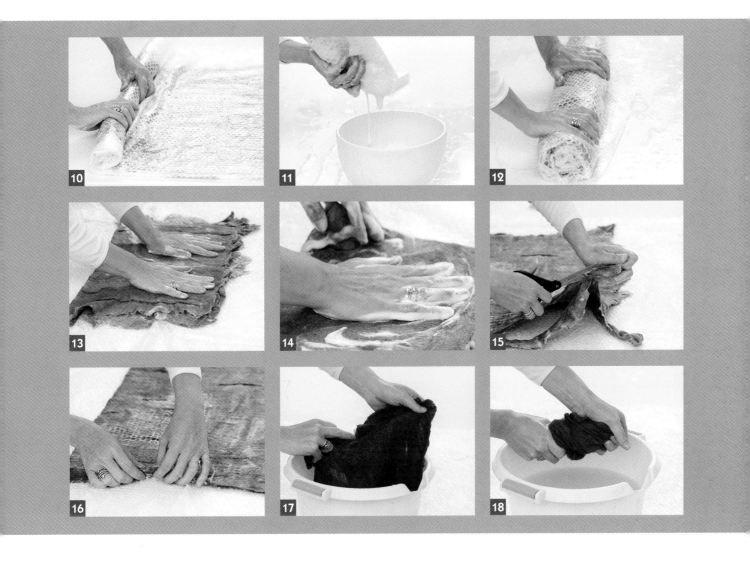

10–11. Roll up the felt in the bubble wrap and, if necessary, drain off the excess water into a bowl.

12. Work the wool by rolling it back and forth. You also need to be patient at this stage. Every so often, unroll the felt and check the progress. Roll the felt back up and continue the felting process.

13. Unroll the wool and double it as shown in the photo. The felting process happens quicker when you only have to work on half the area.

14. Press the wool with more soap and water, making sure that the layers don't felt together. Turn and continue to felt.

15. If the felt will be used for a pillow or a piece with specific dimensions, trim the edges of the felt even.

16. Fold up an edge and felt some more.

17–18. Rinse the felt several times in clear water, and then wring it out. Finish by hanging the felt to dry.

BABY

MOBILE WITH GUARDSMEN

Mobiles are popular gifts for the little ones. Hang one up over the baby blanket or playpen. We'll first show you how to make the little guardsmen—five in all—and then how to felt the ring and hangers.

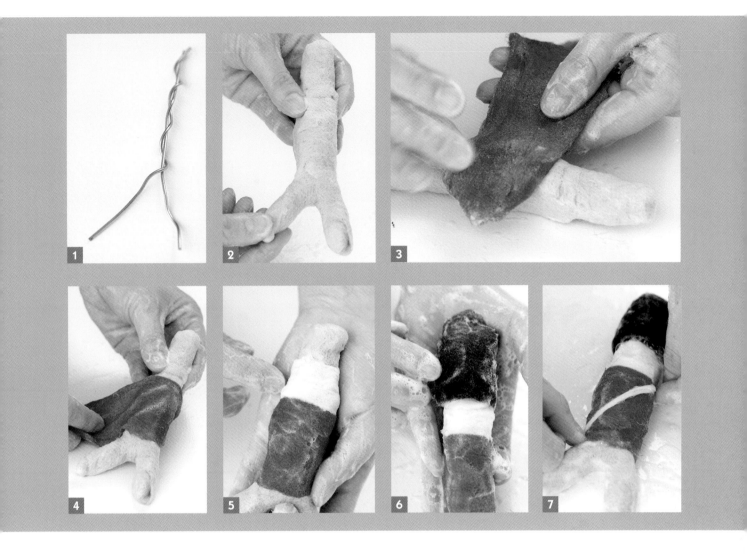

Guardsmen

1. Cut two 4¾"-long pieces of metal wire that's not too thick. Wrap the wire pieces around each other as shown, using pliers if necessary. The two ends that stick out will be the legs.

2. Wrap light blue wool around the wire skeleton, covering the metal thoroughly, and wet it with lukewarm soapy water so that the figure is wet all the way through. Carefully rub and work the wool until it hangs together and the figure is firm. Add soap during the process as necessary.

3. From a piece of red wet felt, cut a little red jacket.

4. Wrap it around the body of the figure. Felt it firmly with repeated motions using water and soap. It's important that the red and light blue layers felt together completely.

5. Make a face by positioning and felting a piece of white felt as for the uniform.

6. Add a piece of black felt for the bearskin hat and felt it thoroughly.

7. Decorate the jacket with strips of white wool and give the figure a final round of felting so that all the layers hold together completely.

When the figure has been rinsed and dried, you can add facial features with embroidery floss or yarn as shown in the illustration opposite and the photo on page 21. Repeat the directions to make a total of five guardsmen, and then make the mobile ring as explained on page 20.

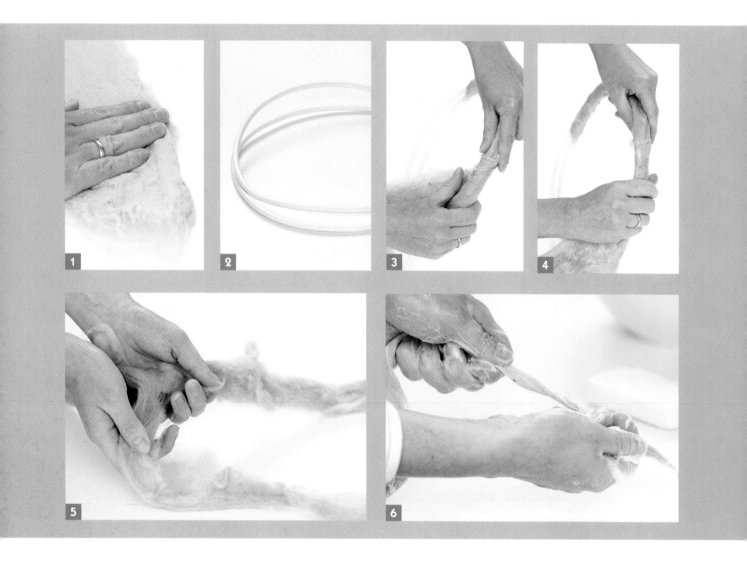

As with all craft projects, make sure to keep these items out of reach of Baby, and make sure all small parts are sewn down securely to avoid a choking hazard.

Felted Ring

This ring is used for the mobile but can have many other uses. For example, you can use the same method to make a smaller piece for a lovely bracelet.

1. Lay a batt of wool on the table and dampen it with soapy water.

2. Use stiff plastic tubing or something similar to form two 9½" diameter rings. The rings can be joined with tape.

3. Wrap the wool around the rings and rub it well, adding soapy water as necessary.

4. Work your way around the ring so that it's completely covered. Be sure that any overlapping is as invisible as possible. Beginning in a different spot, cover the ring with another layer of wool. Continue adding layers until the ring is the desired thickness.

Cords

5. Make a cord by first pulling a thin strip of wool.

6. Dampen the wool and rub it in the soap. Work the wool until it holds together well. Roll it in bubble wrap.

Finishing

When the wool is dry, assemble the mobile as shown above. Using a needle and sturdy thread, attach a short length of black yarn to the top of each guardsman. Attach four of them to the ring and the fifth one to a thick cord in the center. Felt four thick cords of desired length for hanging the mobile.

Hang the floating guardsmen over the baby's blanket or playpen.

Instructions for the felted balls are on page 25, step 4. Attach the balls and cords to the ring and tie the cord ends together in a knot.

BALLS

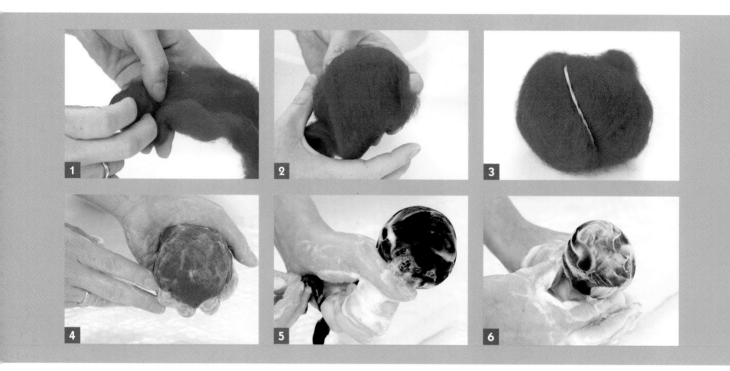

There are endless variations of balls to make and many ways to decorate them. For ideas, see the photo opposite. If you want to save the more expensive dyed wool for later, you can start the ball with undyed wool or something else, such as a wad of newspaper, aluminum foil, or Styrofoam ball. But you'll get the best result when you use wool for the entire piece.

Make the Ball

1–2. Begin by rolling a batt of wool together. Make sure it isn't too tight or too loose. It helps to roll the wool around a little glass or plastic ball or something similar so you can get the right shape. If the ball can be opened, place a little round bell in the center that you can hear when the ball is rolled or rattled.

3. Hold the ball together with a rubber band.

4. Roll another layer of wool around the ball, and then quickly dip it into soapy water. Squeeze the excess water out and shape the piece with your soapy hands.

5. Put the ball into a nylon stocking and rub the whole ball well until the wool begins to cohere. It's important to be patient here. Occasionally take the ball out of the stocking and check the process of the felting.

6. Add soap as necessary.

Decorate the Ball

You can decorate the ball with stars, stripes, or other motifs. Begin by felting a piece of fabric as explained on page 12. The balls can also be decorated with thin wool stripes or shapes in various colors.

7–8. Cut out a star or other shape.

9. Lay the shape on the ball, dampen with soapy water, and straighten and smooth the shape.

10. Cover with curtaining, plastic netting, or organza, and work the ball until the embellishment is thoroughly felted to it. Rinse out well and set out to dry.

BLOCKS

Put a little bell inside the block and it will tinkle.

Just like the balls described on the previous pages, these blocks don't take long to make. You can use ready-made felt fabric for the decorations and sew them with a narrow zigzag stitch, as shown on the block with the star. If you make the felt yourself, you can decorate the blocks in various ways. What about stripes, for example?

Striped Block

1. Lay out the wool on a sheet of bubble wrap as shown on page 12. Add strips of wool in another color. The photo shows diagonal stripes. We've only used two colors, but you can use more colors as shown in the blocks opposite.

2. Saturate the wool with soapy water.

3. Felt and work the wool as explained in "Making Felt" on page 12. Roll the wool in bubble wrap.

Small Felted Balls

The blocks can be embellished with small felted balls.

4. Roll a little ball, thoroughly wet it with soapy water, and work it well until the wool coheres firmly. Don't forget that it will take a little while. Your patience will be rewarded.

5. When the wool is completely felted, use a sharp knife to cut it in half.

6. You'll have two half balls or felted knobs. Rinse the balls and let them dry.

Assembling the Block

For each block, cut six squares about 4¾" x 4¾" each. Decorate each square, sewing the small knobs on by hand. You can sew the stars using a zigzag stitch or felt them onto wet felt as explained on page 55.

Sew the sides with a blanket stitch (see "Blanket Stitch" on page 11), leaving a small opening for the filling. Stuff the block with fiberfill or similar material and sew the opening closed. It's a nice idea to put a little bell in with the filling.

Some of our baby designs are decorated with little guardsmen cut from ready-made felt fabric: a black hat, a white head, a red uniform/body, and light blue legs. The guardsman pattern below will fit on a square about 4¾" x 4¾".

Pin the various pieces in place on the felt square. Then sew them with a narrow zigzag stitch. Lastly, embroider black eyes, a red mouth, and a white cross over the chest.

If you would rather felt the design, you can felt the motifs to the squares by securing them with curtaining, plastic netting, or organza. The easiest sequence is to begin with the hat, then the head, then the uniform/body, and finish with the legs.

TOY BOX

Many of the projects in this book are produced using the same basic techniques and that also applies to the toy boxes here. By varying the decorations, they can be appropriate for all ages—from the youngest to the oldest. A variety of designs are shown in the photos in this book.

If you want to make a toy box quickly and easily, use ready-made felt (see "Resources" on page 127). Of course, you can felt the fabric for the box yourself. Refer to "Making Felt" on page 12.

Cut one 10¼" x 13" base, two 9" x 13" side pieces, two 9" x 10¼" end pieces, and two 1¼" x 6¼" handles. The front can be decorated as shown in the photo with three guardsmen. For each guard, cut a black hat, a white head, a red uniform/body, and light blue legs, using the pattern on page 29 as a guide for sizing the guards. Pin the pieces in place on the felt, and then sew them with a narrow zigzag stitch. Finally, embroider each guardsman with black eyes, a red mouth, and a white cross over the chest.

Sew the handles to each end of the box. With wrong sides together, machine stitch the end pieces between the side pieces, and then sew the box to the base piece. You can also sew the pieces together with a blanket stitch (see "Blanket Stitch" on page 11).

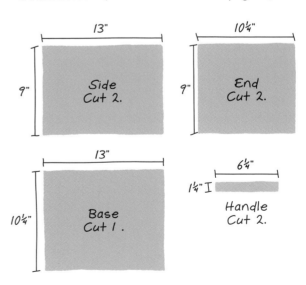

BAGS

These bags (like the one hanging on the right in the photo) are just as useful for storage as the boxes on the previous page. They can also be made from ready-made felt (see "Resources" on page 127).

Cut two 10¼" x 12¼" pieces for the bag front and back; round off the two lower corners as shown. A glass or similar object is a useful template for shaping the corner. Next, cut two 2½" x 12¼" side pieces and one 1½" x 33½" handle.

You can decorate the bag front with two guardsmen. For each guard, cut a black hat, a white

head, a red uniform/body, and light blue legs using the pattern opposite as a guide for sizing the guards. Pin the pieces on the bag front, and then sew with a narrow zigzag stitch. Finish by embroidering black eyes, a red mouth, and a white cross over the chest.

Sew the handle securely to the corners on the bag back. With wrong sides together, machine stitch the side pieces between the bag front and back. Stitch across the bottom, sewing through all layers. You can also sew the pieces together with a blanket stitch (see "Blanket Stitch" on page 11).

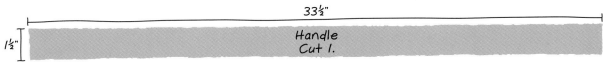

33½"

1½"

Handle
Cut 1.

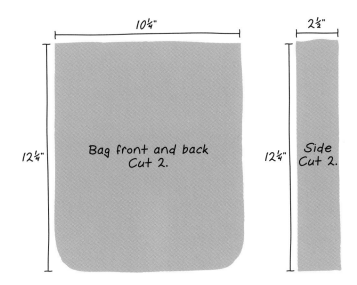

10¼"

2½"

12¼"

Bag front and back
Cut 2.

12¼"

Side
Cut 2.

TEDDY

We decided to allow the teddy into the book even though he isn't felted. This sweet little teddy is sewn from coarse but not heavy fabric. You could use linen, for example.

1. Enlarge and trace the pattern opposite onto a piece of tracing paper to make a paper template. Cut out the pieces, referring to the pattern for color and number of pieces to cut.

2. Place the two front body pieces right sides together and sew the center seam. With right sides together, sew the arms and legs to the corresponding positions on the body front and back pieces. Place the body front and back right sides together and sew,

beginning on the side of the head (directly below where the ear will be) and sewing all the way around to the other side of the head, stopping below where the ear will be.

3. Turn the teddy right side out and stuff with fiberfill through the top of the head. It helps to use a large-sized knitting needle to force the stuffing in place until it's quite firm.

Enlarge patterns 200%.

Ear
Cut 4.

Body back
Cut 1.

Body front
Cut 1 and
1 reversed.

¼" seam allowance

Leg
Cut 4.

4. Sew the ears together in pairs, right sides together, leaving them open at the base. Turn the ears right side out and stuff with fiberfill. Place the ears on top of the head, folding the seam allowances on the front and back of the head under and topstitch.

5. Finish by embroidering the facial features on the teddy.

Arm
Cut 2 and
2 reversed.

PILLOWS

Pillows made from felt are both soft and warm! In this book, you'll find several suggestions for pillows decorated in various ways. Here we have stars and guardsmen which will go with the other pieces in this section—the balls, blocks, toy boxes, and mobile.

For quick and easy pillows, use ready-made felt (see "Resources" on page 127) or make your own felt (see "Making Felt" on page 12). As shown in the photo, the pillows can be edged with crochet (see "Crocheted Edging" on page 11).

Pillow with Guardsmen

1. Cut one 16½" square for the pillow front and two 8½" x 16½" pieces for the pillow back. If the felt is very thick, it's better to use fabric for the pillow back.

2. For each guardsmen, cut a black hat, a white head, a red uniform/body, and light blue legs using the pattern at right as a guide for sizing the guards. Pin the pieces to the pillow front and sew with a narrow zigzag stitch. Finish by embroidering each guardsman with black eyes, a red mouth, and a white cross over the chest.

3. Crochet the edging around the edge of the pillow front, if desired, (see "Crocheted Edging" on page 11).

4. Join the two back pieces with a 16"-long zipper, centering the zipper. Partially open the zipper. Place the pillow front and back right sides together and sew around the edges. If you have a crocheted edging, make sure it's positioned between the front and back before sewing.

5. Turn the pillow right side out through the zipper opening and use a tapestry or knitting needle to poke out the corners. Insert a pillow form.

If you don't want a zipper opening, cut the back the same size as the pillow front. Place the pillow front and back right sides together and sew around edges, leaving a 10" opening for turning. Turn the pillow right side out. Stuff with fiberfill or insert a pillow form and close the opening with small, invisible stitches.

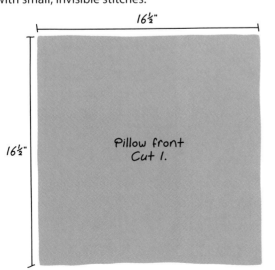

16½"

16½"

Pillow front
Cut 1.

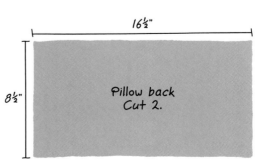

16½"

8½"

Pillow back
Cut 2.

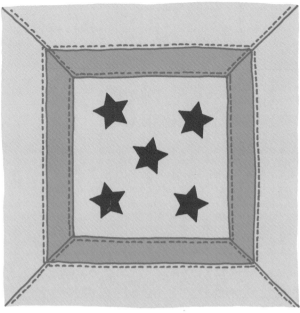

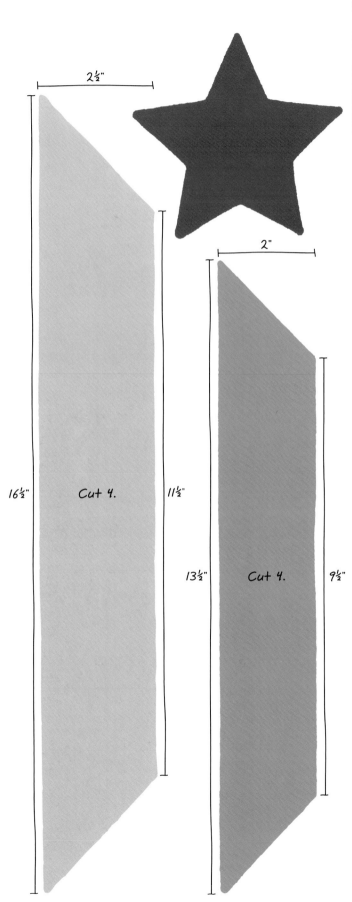

2½"

16½"   Cut 4.   11½"

2"

13½"   Cut 4.   9½"

Pillow with Stars

For this pillow, the front is made from several pieces surrounding a 9½" x 9½" light blue center. Cut out the pieces as indicated on the patterns at left. Sew the dark blue inner border to the center square as shown in the illustration, and then join the light blue outer border. Decorate the center with stars.

If the felt is very thick, use fabric for the pillow back. For the pillow back, cut two 8½" x 16½" pieces and join them with a 16"-long zipper. Partially open the zipper. Place the pillow front and back right sides together and sew around the edges. If you have a crocheted edging, make sure it's positioned between the front and back before sewing. Turn the pillow right side out through the zipper opening and use a tapestry or knitting needle to sharpen the corners. Insert a pillow form.

POLICE CAR

The police car is a big hit with little boys. With a little imagination, the police car can be transformed into many other types of car.

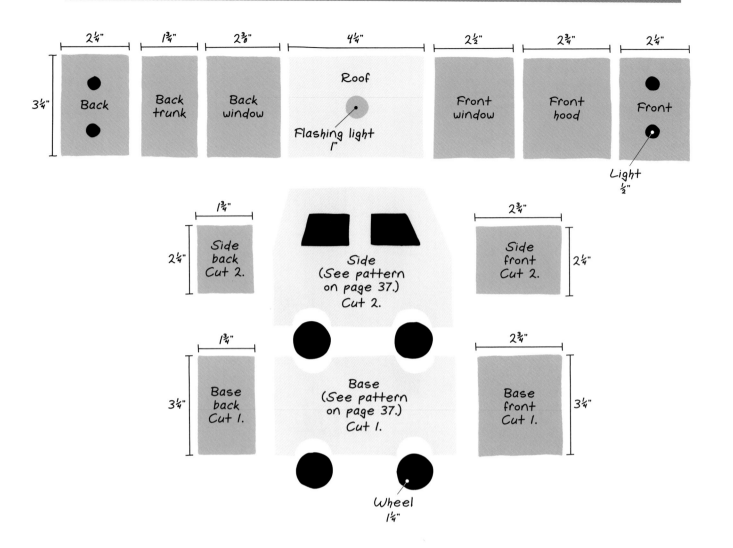

1. Referring to the pattern above and opposite for color and size, cut out the pieces. While the white felt is still wet, you can felt the black windows using the technique on page 55. You can also sew or use fabric glue to attach the windows after the felt is dry.

2. The wording can either be needle felted or embroidered by hand or machine.

3. Felt four black balls for the wheels and one small blue egg-shaped ball for the flashing light (see page 25). After felting the blue ball, cut off the bottom to make it flat and attached it to the car roof.

4. Sew the black lights to the front and back pieces. With wrong sides together, join the pieces with a blanket stitch as shown on page 11. Leave an opening to stuff the car. Stuff with fiberfill and close the opening.

BOX WITH POLICE CAR MOTIF

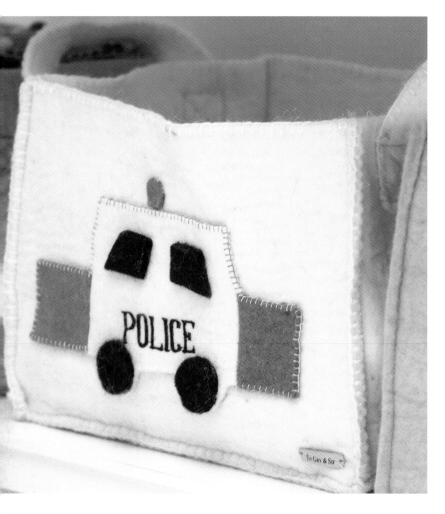

Use the measurements and instructions on page 27 to make the box and decorate the front with a police car using the pattern below. Assemble the police car using one of the following methods.

One method that results in a nice look is to cut the whole car shape (except the blue light on top) from a piece of light blue wet felt. Cut the white car front from a piece of firmly wet-felted fabric. Place the white felt over the blue, and then felt the layers together (see "Making Felt" on page 12). To firm up the felt, roll it in bubble wrap. Felt on the black wheels and windows in the same manner. You can felt or embroider the wording. Rinse the felt car and lay it flat to dry before sewing it to the 10¼" x 13" box front with a blanket stitch (see "Blanket Stitch" on page 11). Be sure to add the blue flashing light on top.

Or, instead of felting the pieces together, you can use ready-made felt and the pattern to cut out light blue, white, and black pieces. Sew the separate pieces to the box front.

Enlarge pattern 200%.

POLICE CAR ON A ROPE

Cut a police car shape from light blue wet felt (see "Making Felt" on page 12). To make the car thick and plump as shown in the photo, lay light blue wool on both sides and around the edges. Use a thick layer of wool, curving it around the corners; felt it, and then roll the car shape in bubble wrap.

When the car is the desired thickness, felt a layer of white wool for the car body as shown in the photo. Work in the white wool by rubbing with water and soap, and then rolling it in bubble wrap. Finish by cutting out black wheels and windows from wet felt and felt them to the car.

For the cord, felt small white balls and light blue balls using the technique on page 25. After they are dry, string them onto a cord as shown and firmly attach the cord to the car.

LONDON BUS

This double-decker London bus is a very popular design. You'll need two colors—red and black. It's easiest to cut out the pieces from dry felt, preferably ready-made (see "Resources" on page 127).

1. Using the patterns below and on pages 42 and 43, cut the bus pieces from a piece of red felt. Cut out the windows and doors from black felt (the doors are only on one side of the bus). Sew or glue the windows and the doors to the bus sides and ends.

2. Embroider or needle felt the wording onto the little sign. Felt four round black balls for the wheels.

3. With wrong sides together, join the pieces with a blanket stitch (see "Blanket Stitch" on page 11). Leave a small opening to stuff the bus. Stuff the bus with fiberfill and close the opening. Sew the sign on the top of the bus.

Side
Cut 2.

Make 8 windows for one side and
6 windows plus 2 doors for the other side.

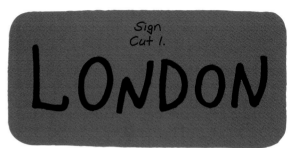

Front and back ends
Cut 2.

Make 2 lights and 2 windows for the front end.
Make 2 lights only for the back end.

Roof
Cut 1.

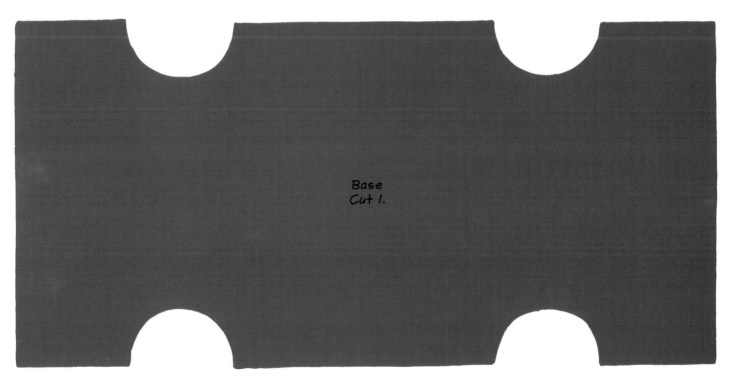

Base
Cut 1.

LITTLE CASES

These little cases have many possible uses: for baby bottles, nursery items, or little toys. You can decorate them in a variety of ways. Make small knobs or striped felt using the techniques on page 25. Other ideas for embellishment can be found on pages 50, 52, and 56. You may want to line the cases.

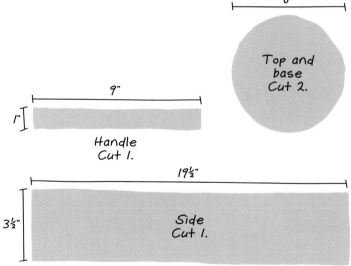

6"

Top and
base
Cut 2.

9"

1"

Handle
Cut 1.

19½"

3½"

Side
Cut 1.

1. Referring to the measurements on the pattern and using a compass or a round object, draw the top and base on a piece of dry felt. Cut out the pieces. You can make the top and base pieces a bit larger or smaller but make sure you adjust the measurements of the side piece as well.

2. Cut out the side piece following the measurements on the pattern. With right sides together, sew the ends together to form a ring to fit between the top and base. Turn the ring right side out and sew it to the base circle.

3. Cut out the handle piece. Overlapping the ends, sew the handle into a ring. Sew it to the top circle as shown to make the lid.

4. Sew a 12" zipper between the lid and the side piece. Finish sewing the lid and side pieces together (where not attached by the zipper).

5. If you want, decorate the zipper by sewing a little felt ball to the pull tab.

KNOBBLY SLIPPERS

These warm slippers would also be sweet if made of light red wool with dark red, yellow, and green knobs.

It's really enjoyable to felt slippers but it also takes a little practice. First, it takes a while for the wool to felt. Second, you'll find that it's easiest to wrap the wool around a rubber boot to shape the slipper. But once you get the hang of it, you'll find its great fun. These slippers are very warm and once one person in the family has a pair, everyone will want one!

If you are going to felt the slippers around rubber boots, use a pair a size larger than the desired slipper size because the wool will shrink as it felts.

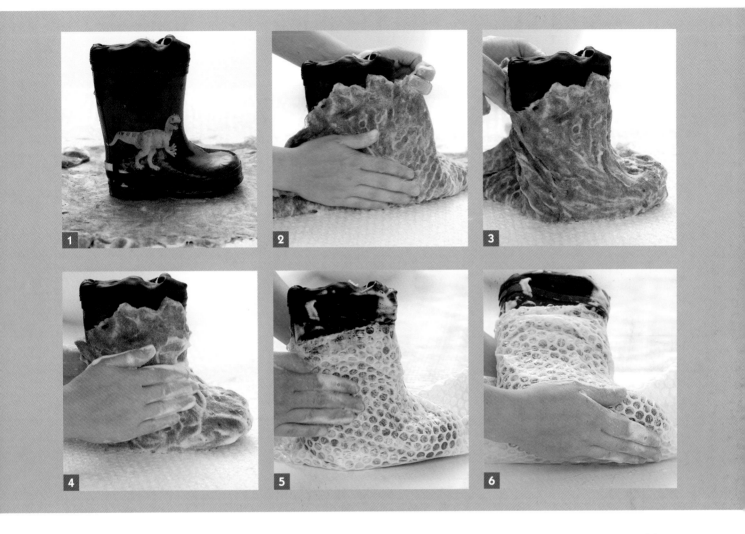

1. Begin by felting a piece of fabric that isn't too thick. Wet felt following the instructions for "Making Felt" on page 12. Center the boot on the felt.

2–3. Wrap the wool around the boot as shown.

4. Rub the felt with soapy water until the wool begins to cohere. The slippers shown in the photo opposite have one color on the inside and another on the outside. You can produce the same effect by adding a layer of wool "shingles" in the second color, overlapping the layers and covering the first color. In the photos above, the slippers are worked with two layers of the same color. The slippers should be a bit thick.

5. Cover the wool with bubble wrap and rub briskly.

6. Rub the bottom of the slipper.

When the wool holds together well, trim the edges and carefully remove the boot. Continue felting with one hand inside the slipper while you rub it on the outside. If you want the slippers to perfectly fit the person for whom they are being made, have him or her try on the wet slippers and continue to felt the outside. When the slippers are completely felted, remove them from the recipient's feet. Rinse and let them dry, making sure they are shaped correctly. Finish by embellishing the slippers with little colored knobs using the technique on page 25.

47

PRINCESS

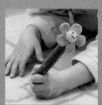

PRINCESS CASE

Felt is the perfect material for little princesses. Of course, pink and rose are the best colors for these projects. Instructions for making a case are on page 44. This one is made with the same method except it's topped with a princess crown.

Cut the crown from a piece of dry felt using the pattern opposite. Sew the crown along the two short sides, and then sew the crown to the top of the case with small, invisible stitches. If you like, decorate the zipper by sewing a little felt ball to the pull tab.

There are many ways to decorate the case. We've decorated the one shown with sequins, but beads also look wonderful.

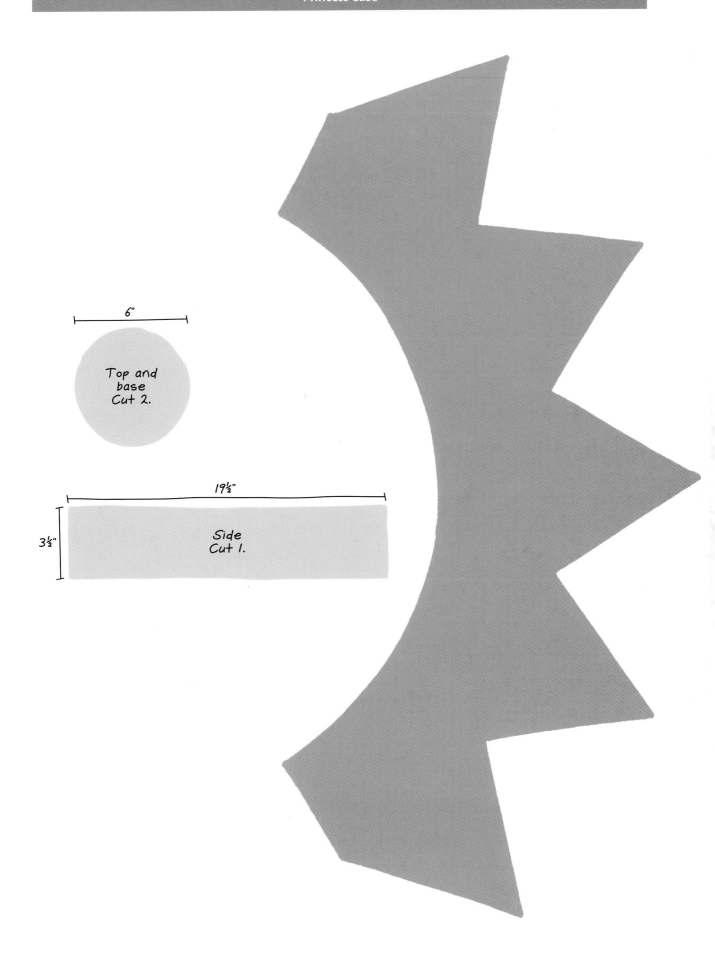

6"

Top and
base
Cut 2.

19½"

3½"

Side
Cut 1.

CASE WITH FLOWERS

Later in this book, we'll show you how to make felt flowers to embellish hairpins (see page 57). Here we use them to decorate the case on the facing page. (Instructions for making a case are on page 44.) The little flowers are securely sewn to the side of the case with a bead or sequin. The same size flower can also be attached to the zipper pull tab. The large flower for the lid is embellished with a felted ball that has a face embroidered on it. Place the ball in the center of the flower and sew it securely to the lid as shown.

BOX WITH HEARTS

A box with hearts is perfect for storing what one holds dearest.

For many of the designs in this book, the decorative element is sewn on with narrow zigzag stitches. However, the embellishments can also be felted on as done in this project. In order to do this, it's very important that both the embellishment and the felted fabric base are kept wet.

1. Cut out a heart or other desired shape from wet felt. You might want to use a template. Lay it on the wet felt and mark the outline with a knitting needle or something similar. This will leave an impression in the wet felt.

2. Making sure that the right side is facing up so the pieces will match, place the heart on the felt background and press it in well.

3. Cover with curtaining, plastic netting, or organza so that the heart is held in place. Rub it all over with water and soap until the embellishment is firmly felted to the background. Roll in bubble wrap and work it a little while longer.

When the felt is dry, decorate the hearts with sequins or beads as shown. Use the measurements and instructions on page 27 to make the box. Join the pieces and then embellish with a blanket stitch (see "Blanket Stitch" on page 11).

CASE WITH HEARTS

Here is another version of the case using the measurements and instructions on page 44. On page 55, we explain how to felt the heart decorations. Use the patterns to felt a little heart on the case and attach a felted heart to the zipper pull tab. Sew a 1" x 9" handle to the lid.

HAIRPIN WITH FLOWERS

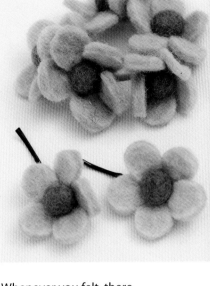

Whenever you felt, there are always a lot of small remnants. These can be cut into flower petals and formed into several kinds of hair decorations.

Scrunchie

Cut out a handful of flower petals from dry felt and sew them together. Felt several little balls and sew a ball in the center of each flower. Sew the flowers onto an elastic ponytail band.

Hairpin

For each hairpin, use one flower and one ball for the center. Sew the pieces together, and then sew a hairpin to the back. It's that easy!

PENCIL HOLDER

Almost any kind of pencil can be decorated with a felt pencil holder.

1. Lay out one layer of wool. Lay a second layer perpendicularly on top of the first layer. Saturate the wool with water and soap.

2. Trim the edges evenly.

3. Fold the edge and roll the felt around a pencil.

4. Roll the pencil back and forth on the table over a piece of bubble wrap until the wool begins to hold together as a tube. If you want the tube to be striped, add another color of wool.

5. Roll the felt and pencil in a piece of bubble wrap and continue to felt until the tube is very firm. Let dry with the pencil inside.

The photos on this page and on page 60 show how the holders can be decorated. Enlarge the patterns opposite and use them to cut wings and flowers from dry felt. Use fine yarn or embroidery floss for the insect antennae and knot as shown; embroider the eyes. Sew a felt ball in the center of each flower and embroider the eyes and mouth with black floss.

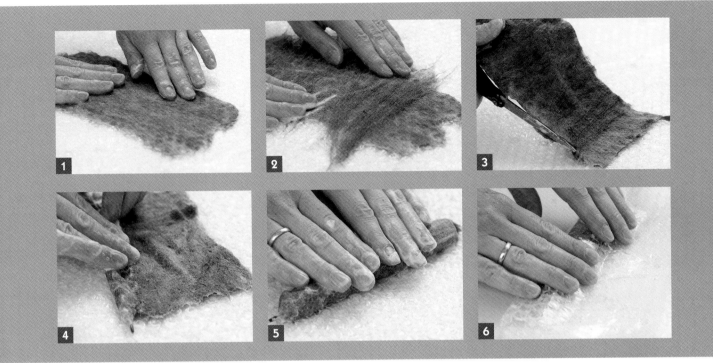

Enlarge patterns 125%.

BAG WITH POCKETS

This bag is perfect for toting the pencil holders shown on page 58.

1. Cut out all the pieces using the measurements shown on the illustration. We've also included color suggestions. Use the heart template to cut three hearts from dry felt. Divide the pocket into three sections as indicated on the pattern. Place the hearts on the pocket and machine stitch them in place. Topstitch along the pocket's top edge. Place the pocket on the bag front and sew it securely by first sewing the two vertical center lines, and then sewing the ends. Stitch along the pocket's bottom edge.

2. Sew a 1¼" x 1½" piece to each short end of a 9"-long zipper. Sew a 1½" x 11¾" piece to each long side of the zipper. This makes the top of the bag.

3. Place the top of the bag and the bag front wrong sides together. Insert the ends of one handle between the two pieces as shown in the photo opposite and machine stitch. Repeat for the bag back. Sew the sides and base between the front and back pieces. Blanket stitch as shown in the photo (see "Blanket Stitch" on page 11). Don't forget to sew a blanket stitch along the sides of the handles.

If you want, put some pencil holders into the pockets as shown.

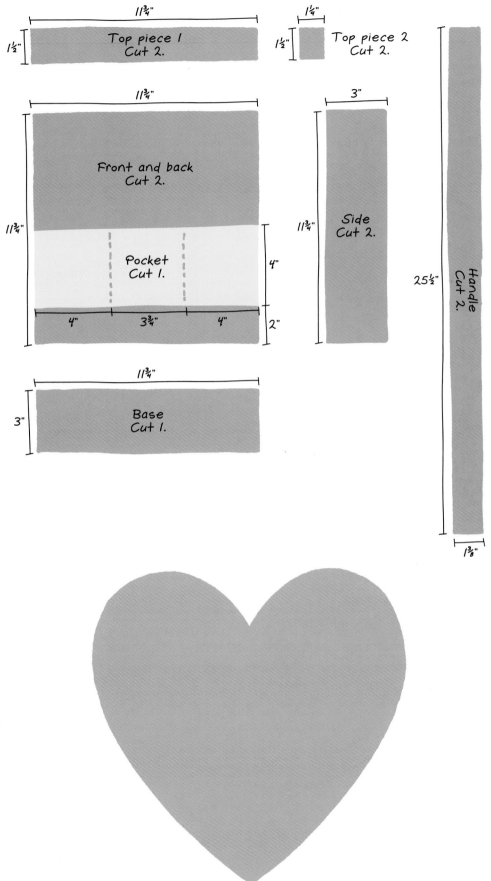

FINGER PUPPETS

The finger puppets are made the same way as the pencil holders on page 58. If you are successful at making the holders, then these finger puppets will be easy.

1. Make a piece of felt as instructed on page 12, but stop felting before it's too firm. Take the tube off the pencil and trim it so that it's the length of a finger. Carefully try on the tube through the open end.

2. Felt the edge well.

3. Put the tube on a finger and felt the tube while on a finger. Finish by rinsing the tube and letting it dry.

Use the patterns opposite to cut out wings and a flower from dry felt. Use fine yarn or embroidery floss for the insect antennae and knot as shown; add black beads for eyes. Embellish the flower head with a round felt ball. Add black beads for eyes and embroider a mouth.

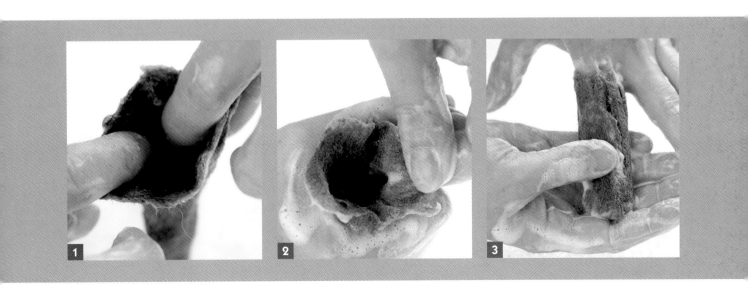

HORSES

Large Horse

The felt for the large horse in the photo has green spots encircled by a pink ring. Make the spots by following the instructions on page 55 while the felt is wet.

1. Enlarge and copy the patterns on pages 66 and 67. Use the patterns to cut two side pieces, an underside with legs, a forehead gusset, and four ears.

2. With right sides together, sew the ears together in pairs and turn them right side out. Place the ears on the right side of the forehead gusset with the tips toward the center and sew securely. With right sides together, sew the forehead to one side piece. Leaving an opening under the neck, sew the two side pieces together from the neck, around the muzzle, and up over the back.

3. Place the sides and underside right sides together and sew all the way around.

4. Turn right side out, stuff the horse firmly with wool using a knitting needle to help pack the wool filling, and then close the underside of the neck with small invisible stitches.

5. Cut a handful of yarn strands, each about 11¾" long; fold them in half and sew them to the horse for the tail. Cut twice as many 9¾" long strands for the mane and sew them securely along the center of the forehead gusset. Embroider the eyes and mouth with black yarn.

Little Horse

The little horse is a simplified version of the larger one. There is no forehead gusset and each ear is only one layer. The ears are sewn securely on each side of the head, after the horse has been stuffed. Use the patterns on page 68 to cut two side pieces, one underside piece, and two ears. With wrong sides together and using a blanket stitch (see "Blanket Stitch" on page 11), hand sew the little horse, leaving an opening for stuffing. Stuff with fiberfill and close the opening. The yarn strands for the tail are about 3¼" long and about 4" for the mane. Fold the strands in half and sew them to the horse after it's been sewn and stuffed. Embroider the eyes and mouth with black yarn, or attach beads for the eyes.

We all love soft little animals in many colors and funny patterns.

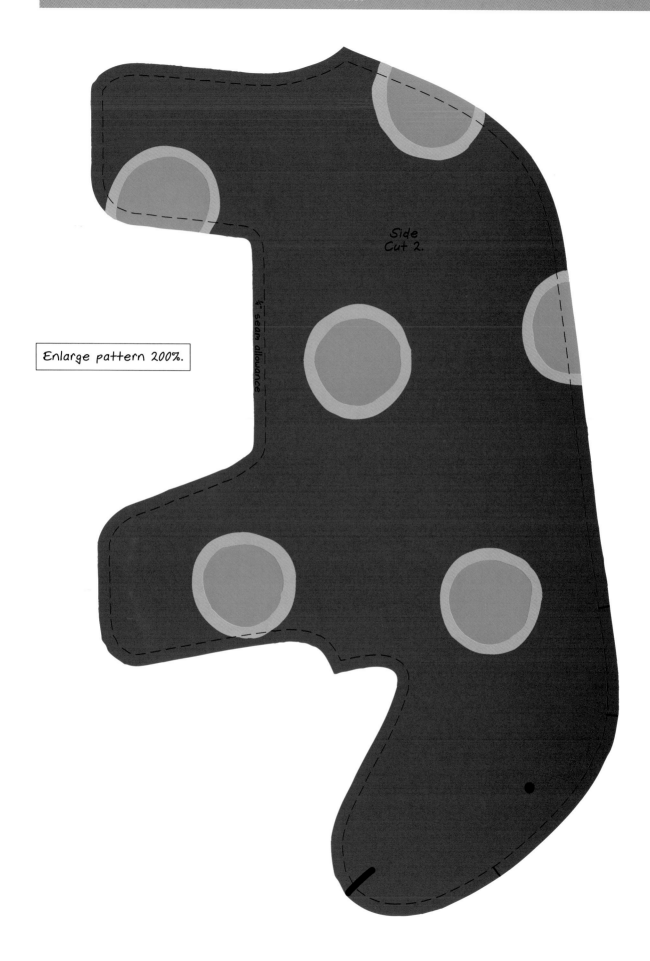

Side
Cut 2.

Enlarge pattern 200%.

¼" seam allowance

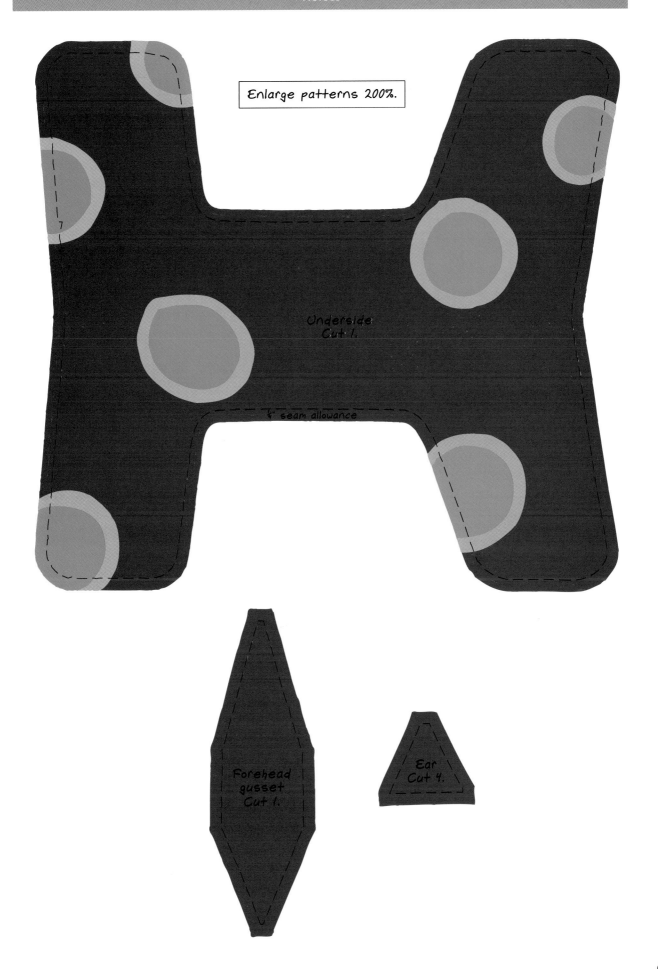

Enlarge patterns 200%.

Underside
Cut 1.

¼" seam allowance

Forehead
gusset
Cut 1.

Ear
Cut 4.

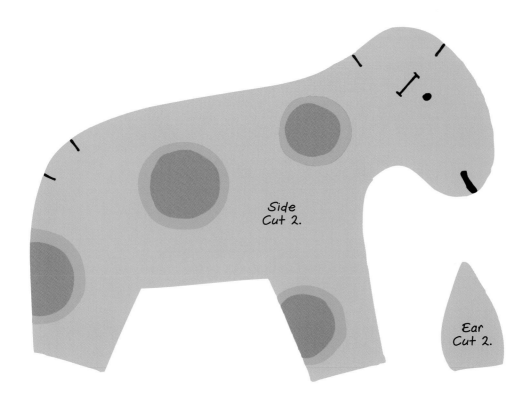

Side
Cut 2.

Ear
Cut 2.

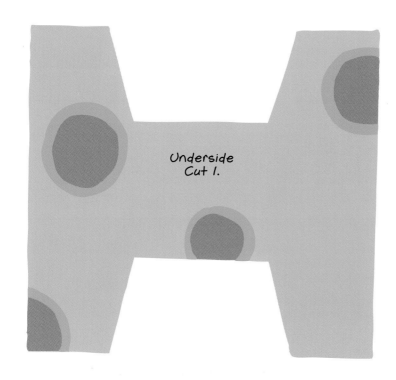

Underside
Cut 1.

KISS THE FROG

... and see if it will become a prince!

Enlarge and copy the patterns opposite. Cut the number of pieces for each color as indicated.

1. With right sides together, sew the curved edge of the lips to the top and bottom of the body, sewing between the two white marks. With right sides together, sew the legs to the top and bottom body pieces. Fold the legs out.

2. Place the top and bottom of the body right sides together. Sew all the way around the body, leaving an opening to turn the frog right side out. Sew the straight edge of the lips together. Turn the frog right side out and stuff with wool using a knitting needle to help pack the wool filling. Close the opening with small invisible stitches. Use an overcast stitch to sew both sides of the mouth between the white and dark markings.

3. Use the technique on page 25 to make two white half balls and sew them to the top of the head for eyes. Embroider black pupils as shown. Choose a crown and cut out one crown piece. Use the wider, straight pattern to make the tall crown seen on page 69. Use the shorter, curved pattern to make the short crown seen above. Sew the ends of the crown piece together and sew it securely to the head.

Enlarge patterns 200%.

Lips
Cut 2.

Crown
Cut 1.

Crown
Cut 1.

¼" seam allowance

Body top and bottom
Cut 1 pink and 1 tan.

Front leg
(top piece)
Cut 2.

Front leg
(bottom piece)
Cut 2.

Back leg
(bottom piece)
Cut 2.

Back leg
(top piece)
Cut 2.

71

RUNNER

To make this runner with hopscotch squares you'll need a large working area and a large piece of bubble wrap. If you have a tile or linoleum floor, you might find it easiest to lay the wool out on the floor. Lay out enough wool to cover an area about 41" x 110" so that the runner will finish to about 31½" x 82½" (after felting).

Referring to "Making Felt" on page 12, lay out layers of dark pink wool, arranging the fibers in four layers and alternating the direction of each layer so that the runner isn't too thin. Felt as instructed, but only until the wool holds together—do not felt thoroughly. Neatly trim the edges.

Lay out rose wool to cover an area about 33½" x 102½". Felt the fabric until it begins to cohere. Do not felt it completely at this point. Trim the edges straight.

Center the rose fabric on top of the dark pink, and then felt the two layers together. Finish with a dark pink border about 3¼" wide.

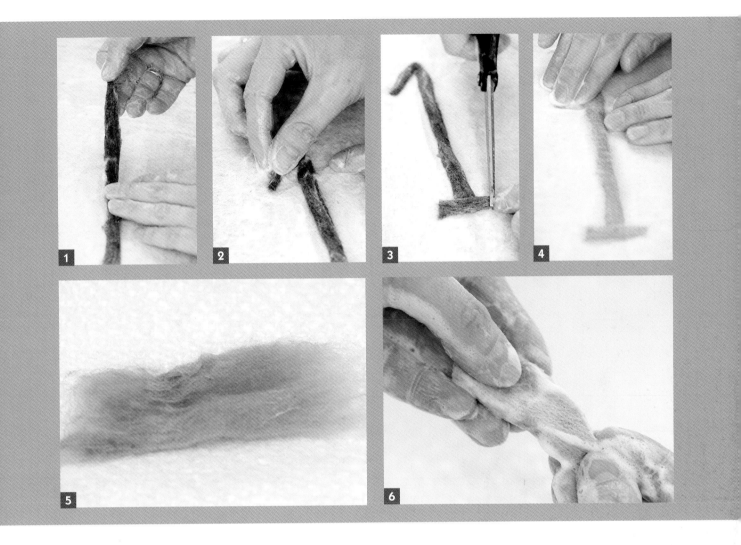

Hopscotch Squares

Add squares to the runner as shown in the illustration on page 74. The lines and numbers are thin strips of wool that are laid out, and then felted. The dimensions shown in the illustration are for the finished project. Use them as a guideline, but make your squares and numbers slightly larger to allow shrinkage.

1. Pull out the wool and carefully press it into the wet base.

2. Adding extra water and soap, shape each number.

3. Neatly trim the edges.

4. Lay curtaining, plastic netting, or organza over the felt so that the numbers are held in place. Now work in more soap and water and felt until the numbers are firmly attached.

Fringe

Decorate the runner by adding fringe all around the edges (see the photo opposite). Begin by carefully cutting along the edge of the runner so that the fringe can be inserted between the layers.

5. Place a piece of pink wool on bubble wrap and wet it with soap and water.

6. Work the wool into a flat piece that holds together well but is loose at one end. Place the loose end between the layers of the runner and felt together under curtaining, plastic netting, or organza. To obtain a smoothly covered edge around the runner, we suggest laying wool tufts all the way around the edge, and then securely felting them together with the fringe.

Let the runner dry, and then sew felted balls to the ends of the fringe.

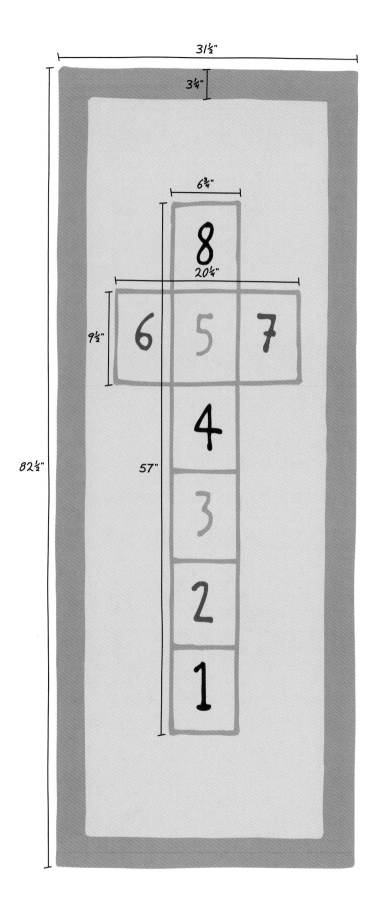

SAWTOOTH-EDGED WASTEPAPER BASKET

To make this felted waste-paper basket, you'll need a bubble-wrap template and a bucket to shape the felt over.

Start by cutting out the bubble-wrap template using the measurements shown on page 76. Referring to "Making Felt" on page 12, lay out the wool, arranging the fibers in four layers and alternating the direction of each layer. Felt the fabric only until it begins to cohere. Cut out the felt using the bubble-wrap template, adding 2" along all sides except the top. Place the template over the felt and fold the extra 2" over the bubble wrap. Cover the rest of the template with felt as described on pages 12 and 13. You now have two layers of felt with the template between them. Continue to work the seams together.

Remove the template and felt the sides well. Place the felted basket over a bucket that is slightly smaller than the basket.

1. Rub and press the wool with soapy hands until the basket shrinks around the bucket.

2. Trim the edge evenly.

3. Cut the sawtooth edge using the triangle pattern below. Rinse the wool and let it dry over the bucket. Finish by decorating with felted balls as shown.

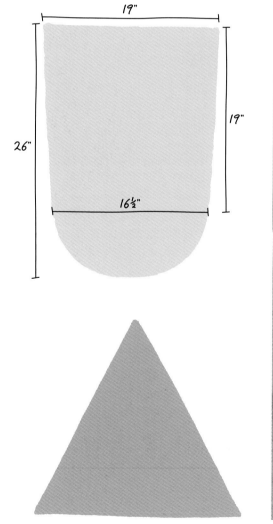

BOX WITH PRINCESS CROWNS

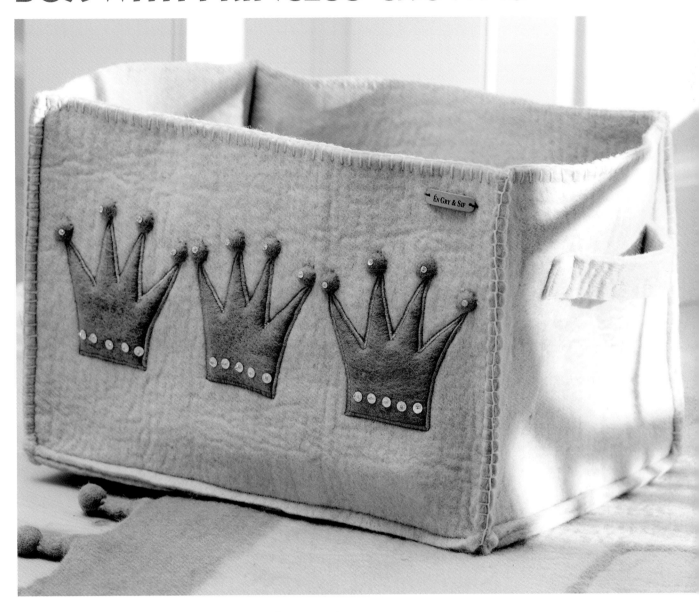

A box for the princess's most treasured possessions.

Here's another box we made using the instructions and measurements on page 27. This box is decorated with three princess crowns that are cut from dry felt fabric using the pattern on page 78. Place the crowns on the box front and sew in place with narrow zigzag stitching. For each crown, make four felted half balls using the technique on page 25 and sew them securely over the points of the crown. Finish by embellishing with sequins or beads as shown.

Instead of sewing the crowns to the box, you could felt them to the felt base using the technique on page 55. For this technique, both the felt base and the crowns must be wet. Place the crowns over the felt base and cover it with curtaining, plastic netting, or organza to hold the crowns in place. Begin by rubbing soapy water into the layers, and then roll the piece in bubble wrap to harden the felt.

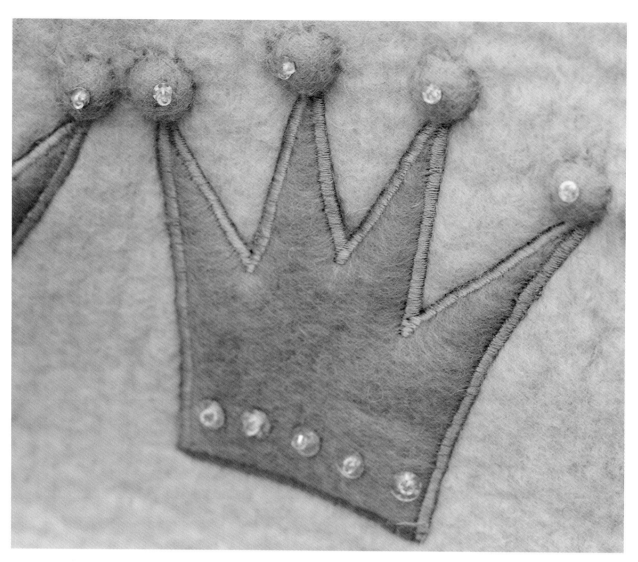

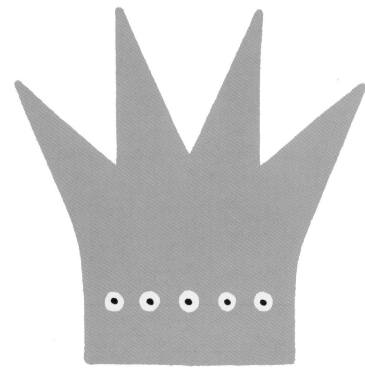

PILLOW WITH CROWN

A pink crown with beads and sequins—a necessity for the bedroom of any princess.

1. Cut one 16½" square for the pillow front and two 8½" x 16½" pieces for the back. Instead of using felt for the backing, you could cut the pieces from knit or other fabric as shown in the photo on page 80. If you use knit fabric, machine stitch along all the edges to prevent unraveling.

2. Using the pattern on page 81, cut out a crown and pin it in place in the center of the pillow front. Sew the crown with a narrow zigzag stitch. Felt four half balls as instructed on page 25 and sew them to the points of the crown as shown. Embellish with sequins or beads. Crochet the edging around the edge of the pillow front, if desired, referring to page 11 as needed. If the back is knit fabric, crochet the edging to the back after the pillow is turned right side out (see photo below).

3. Join the two back pieces with a 16"-long zipper. Partially open the zipper. Place the pillow front and back right sides together and sew around the edges. If you have a crocheted edging, make sure it's positioned between the front and back before sewing.

4. Turn the pillow right side out through the zipper opening and use a tapestry or knitting needle to poke out the corners. Insert a pillow form.

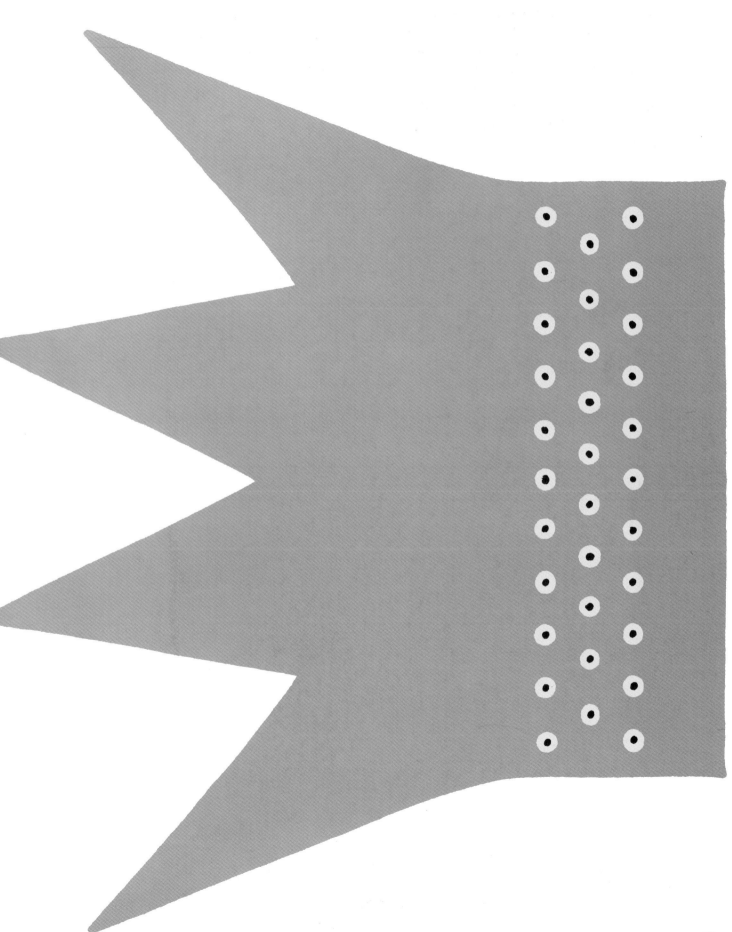

BAG WITH CROWN

This bag has a zipper closure along the top.

1. Cut out all the pieces using the measurements shown on the illustration. Use the pattern on page 85 to cut a crown from dry felt. Pin the crown in place on the bag front and sew with a narrow zigzag stitch. Felt four half balls using the technique on page 25 and sew them to each point of the crown as shown. Embellish with sequins or beads.

2. Sew a 1⅛" x 1¼" piece to each end of an 8"-long zipper. Sew a 1¼" x 10¼" piece to each long side of the zipper. This makes the top of the bag.

3. Place the top of the bag and the bag front wrong sides together. Insert the ends of one handle between the two pieces and machine stitch as shown in the photo opposite. Repeat for the bag back. Sew the sides and base between the bag front and back, and then blanket stitch as shown in the photo (see "Blanket Stitch" on page 11). Don't forget to blanket stitch along the sides of the handles.

Decorate the zipper by sewing a little felt ball to the pull tab.

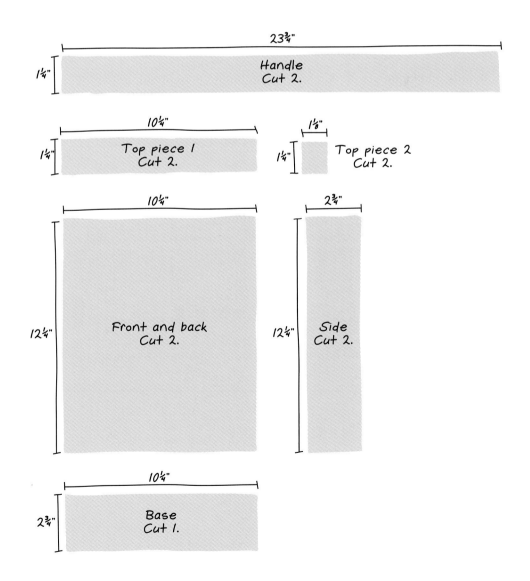

23¾"

Handle
Cut 2.

1¼"

10¼"

Top piece 1
Cut 2.

1¼"

1⅛"

Top piece 2
Cut 2.

1¼"

10¼"

Front and back
Cut 2.

12¼"

2¾"

Side
Cut 2.

12¼"

10¼"

Base
Cut 1.

2¾"

LOVE

PILLOW WITH GRAPHIC DESIGNS

This book contains several square pillows but it's also nice to have pillows in other shapes. How about a rectangle?

The illustrations opposite list the measurements for both square and rectangular pillows. The backs are joined, respectively, with 16"-long and 20"-long zippers. Instructions for making the pillows are on pages 79 and 80.

It's fun to experiment with various graphic forms, and, as shown here, it's very simple. You can also make something even wilder looking.

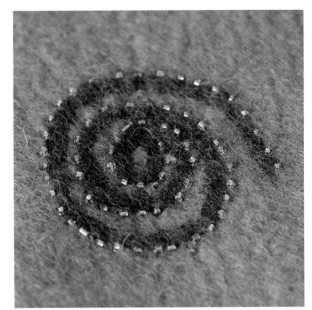

The large polka dots are cut from light green wet felt and wet felted on using the technique on page 55. It's important that the fabric for the spots is cut thin enough so that the pattern will look transparent. When the felt has dried, decorate it with small beads as shown.

You can easily felt a spiral using hand-felting needles. The wool for the spiral is thinned, and then needle felted onto the dry felt fabric. You can also wet felt a spiral. Embellish the spiral by sewing on beads as shown in the photo.

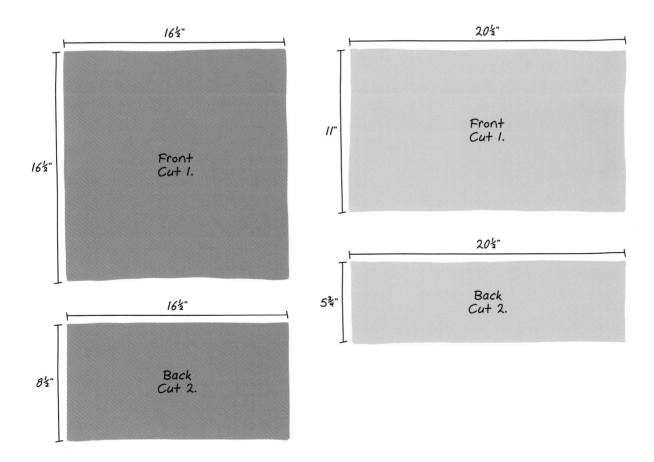

16½"

16½"

Front
Cut 1.

20½"

11"

Front
Cut 1.

16½"

8½"

Back
Cut 2.

20½"

5¾"

Back
Cut 2.

BAG WITH SPOTS

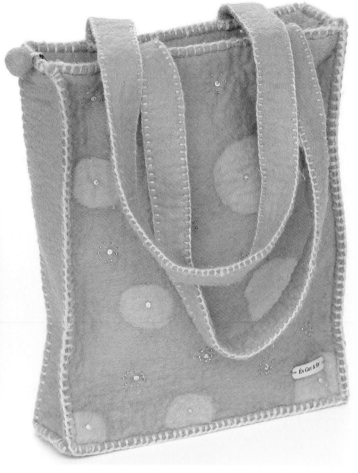

Cut out all the pieces using the measurements shown on the illustration. Sew a 1¹⁄₈" x 1¼" piece to each end of an 8"-long zipper. Sew a 1¼" x 10¼" piece to each long side of the zipper. This makes the top of the bag.

Place the top of the bag and the bag front wrong sides together. Insert the ends of one handle between the two pieces and machine stitch along the long edges. Repeat for the bag back. Sew the sides and base between the front and back, and then blanket stitch as shown in the photo (see "Blanket Stitch" on page 11). Don't forget to blanket stitch along the sides of the handles. Decorate the zipper pull tab with a little felted ball.

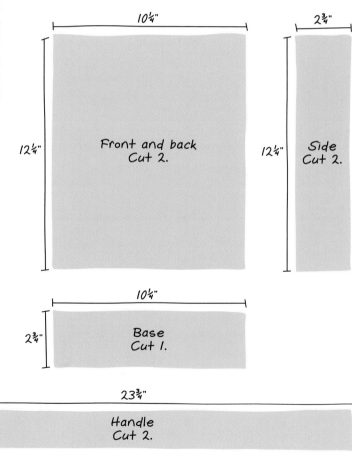

BOX WITH LETTERS

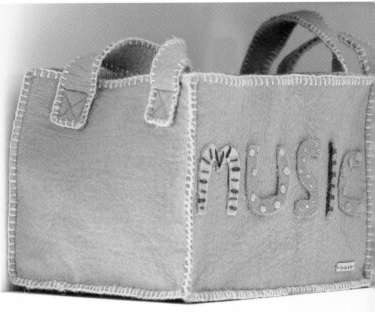

When children reach a certain age, they usually think it's fun to have lettering on their belongings. How about making some boxes with words that indicate what's inside?

Cut and sew the boxes using the measurements and technique on page 27. Note, however, that the handles are made a bit differently here. Cut two 1½" x 12" strips. Blanket stitch along the sides of the handles (see "Blanket Stitch" on page 11). Machine stitch them to the ends of the box with a large X for stability.

Letters

The letters for these boxes are cut from various colors of felt using the alphabet patterns on pages 94–97 and enlarging them by 125%. Sew the letters in place with a narrow zigzag stitch or use fabric glue. The letters can be decorated with small stripes, dots, beads, and other materials as shown in the photo above. Later in this book, you'll find other items that feature these letters as well.

ABC
DEFG
HIJK

For the Box with Letters, Love Pillow, Love Box, Black and Blue Pillows, and Cool Box, enlarge the alphabet patterns 125%.
For the Book Cover, reduce the alphabet patterns 94%.

LMN OPQ RSTU

For the Box with Letters, Love Pillow, Love Box, Black and Blue Pillows, and Cool Box, enlarge the alphabet patterns 125%.
For the Book Cover, reduce the alphabet patterns 94%.

For the Box with Letters, Love Pillow, Love Box, Black and Blue Pillows, and Cool Box, enlarge the alphabet patterns 125%.
For the Book Cover, reduce the alphabet patterns 94%.

1 2 3 4

5 6 7

8 9 0

For the Box with Letters, Love Pillow, Love Box, Black and Blue Pillows, and Cool Box, enlarge the number patterns 125%.
For the Book Cover, reduce the number patterns 94%.

MAKE-UP BAG

If you have some felt remnants, you can make this small and stylish make-up bag. The felt we used here is left over from one of the pillows shown on page 90.

Cut two 5½" x 8¼" pieces and join them along one edge with an 8"-long zipper. With wrong sides together, sew around the remaining three sides with a blanket stitch (see "Blanket Stitch" on page 11). You can also sew the blanket stitch decoratively along the two edges of the zipper as shown. Embellish the pull tab with a felt ball. Line the bag if desired.

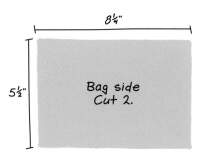

8¼"

5½"

Bag side
Cut 2.

CANDLE COVERS

Glass covered with wool gives a very nice effect when the fabric contains holes. As the flame burns down in the glass, the light glimmers partly through the wool and partly through the holes.

There are two ways to make these covers. The easiest way is to cut pieces of felt long enough to fit around the candle holder plus ½" for seam allowances.

Use a knife to cut various sizes of holes. With right sides together, sew the fabric into a tube that will fit snugly over the candle holder. If you want to avoid sewing, you can felt the cover using the method for the wastepaper basket on page 75. Cut a template from thick plastic, tapering the piece to match the candle cover. Complete by felting around the candle holder.

ELEPHANT

This elephant can be made in all sorts of colors.
With his striped blanket, this little guy is very exotic.

1. Use the patterns to cut two side pieces, one underside piece, and two ears.

2. With wrong sides together, place the underside between the two side pieces. Using a blanket stitch (see "Blanket Stitch" on page 11), hand sew the pieces together, leaving an opening for stuffing. Stuff with fiberfill and close the opening.

3. Edge the ears with a blanket stitch and sew them to each side of the head.

4. Cut out the blanket (to make a felted striped blanket, use the technique on page 55). Place the blanket over the body and stitch in place as shown in the photo opposite. Embroider the eyes with black yarn, or attach beads for eyes.

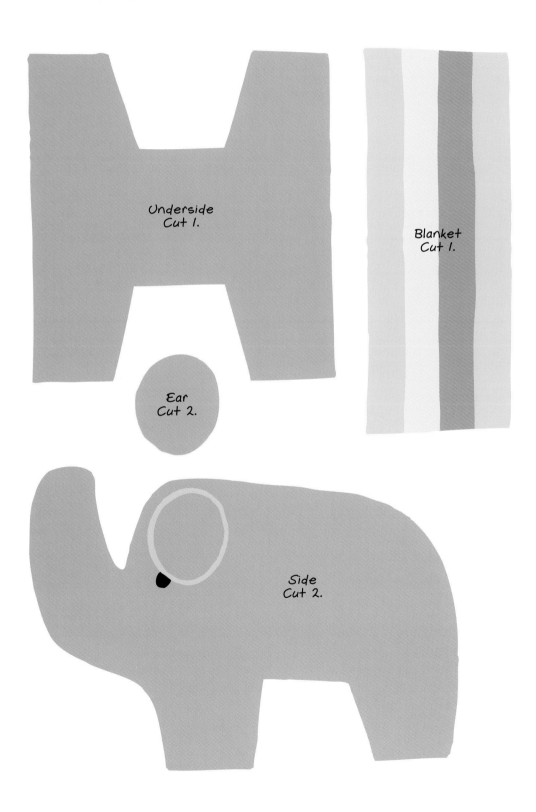

Underside
Cut 1.

Blanket
Cut 1.

Ear
Cut 2.

Side
Cut 2.

LOVE PILLOW

It's fun to have several items that coordinate for your room.
The theme for our ensemble is the word *LOVE*.

Enlarge the alphabet patterns on pages 94–97 by 125%. Use the patterns and felt fabric to cut out letters in shades of pink and rose. You can decorate the letters as shown in the photo opposite. Sew or use fabric glue to attach the letters to the front of the pillow. The front of the rectangular pillow in the photo measures 11" x 20½". The back is made from two 5¾" x 20½" pieces and joined with a 20"-long zipper. Sew the edges with a blanket stitch (see "Blanket Stitch" on page 11). Instructions for making a pillow are on pages 79 and 80.

LOVE BOX

Here's another version of the box made in previous projects. Cut one 10¼" x 13" base piece, two 10¼" x 13" side pieces, and two 9" x 10¼" end pieces. Cut two 1½" x 13¾" handles. Using the alphabet patterns on pages 94–97 and enlarging them by 125%, cut out letters and decorate the box as shown.

Sew or use fabric glue to attach the letters to the box front. Sew the box wrong sides together with a blanket stitch, referring to page 11 for more detailed instructions as needed. Machine stitch the handles to the ends of the box with a large X for stability.

SMALL ROUND CASE

You'll find countless ways to decorate this little case. This one has felted spirals embellished with beads on the top and sides.

1. Referring to the measurements on the illustration opposite and using a compass or a round object, draw the top and base on a piece of dry felt. Cut out the pieces.

2. Cut out the side piece following the measurements on the illustration and, with right sides together, sew the ends together to form a ring to fit between the top and base. Turn the ring right side out and sew it to the base circle.

3. Cut out the handle piece. Sew the handle to the lid as shown in the photo on page 105.

4. Sew a 12" zipper between the lid and the side pieces. Finish sewing the lid and side pieces together (where not attached by the zipper). Blanket stitch the edges as shown in the photo (see "Blanket Stitch" on page 11).

5. If you like, decorate the zipper by sewing a little felt ball to the pull tab.

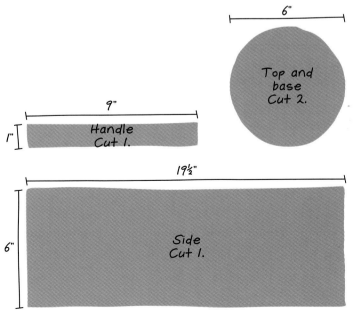

6"

Top and
base
Cut 2.

9"

1" Handle
Cut 1.

19½"

6" Side
Cut 1.

ÉN GRY & SIF

BOOK COVER

This book cover can protect an address book, a diary, or a favorite book.

This cover fits a 6" x 8¼" book. If your book is larger or smaller, adjust the measurements by measuring the book across the front, over the spine, and across the back. Then measure the book's height.

   With wrong sides together and using a blanket stitch (see "Blanket Stitch" on page 11), sew the end flaps to the inside of the cover along each end. Using the alphabet patterns on pages 94–97 and reducing the letters by 94%, cut out the letters to spell out *LOVE*. Decorate the letters as shown. Sew or use fabric glue to attach the letters to the front cover.

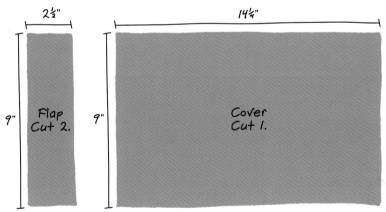

2½"

14¾"

9"

Flap
Cut 2.

9"

Cover
Cut 1.

JEWELRY

Felting offers many possibilities for making jewelry. We'll show you how to felt bracelets, hairpins, and necklaces that you can make as a matching set.

Bracelet

It takes a little practice to felt a ring but it's easier if you felt around a rounded shape, such as a stiff band, tube, or cord. Felting the overlapping areas will take the most practice so that the "seam" will be invisible. Use the technique on page 20 and a single band or cord. Work the beginning and end of the felt ring together with smoothing motions and very soapy hands. As you will see, the felt will suddenly come together. Decorate as you wish, perhaps with beads as shown. You can also embellish a bracelet with felt flowers.

Hairpin

Use the pattern to cut a flower from felt remnants and decorate it with beads or a small felt ball as shown.

Short Necklace

Combine felted balls with small glass beads as shown in the photo at right. Begin by stringing a few glass beads, a large felted ball, and then more glass beads. Finish the chain with a clasp.

Long Necklace

If you are patient and felt a lot of balls you can make a long necklace by stringing balls on a heavy thread, alternating the balls with small glass beads. It is also nice to combine large felted balls with large beads as shown. You might want to decorate some of the felt balls with small beads.

WASTEPAPER BASKET WITH SPIRAL MOTIFS

This wastepaper basket is decorated with spiral motifs after it has been felted and shaped using the technique on pages 75 and 76. On this basket, the edges are trimmed straight instead of using the sawtooth edge on the previous wastepaper basket. The spirals are needle felted, and then embellished with beads. Another design idea is to decorate the wastepaper basket with green polka dots as shown on page 91.

ELF SLIPPERS

Felt these slippers using the technique on pages 46 and 47. To get the two-tone effect, first make a piece of beige felt and shape it around a boot (see photos 1–4 on page 47). Felt the wool firmly around the boot, and then lay the pink wool over the beige so that the beige is completely covered. Continue as instructed on page 47, but keep the wool higher on the boot and trim the edges using the triangle pattern. When the slippers are dry, fold down the top and embellish the points with beads.

COOL

DESK SET

You'll need just black and white felt for these projects. The simple colorway emphasizes the cool look.

Covered Containers

Referring to the measurements on the illustration and using a compass or a round object, draw the top and base on a piece of dry felt. Cut out the pieces. Cut out the side piece following the measurements on the illustration and, with right sides together, sew the ends together to form a ring to fit between the top and base. Turn the ring right side out and sew it to the base circle. Cut out the handle piece. Sew it on the lid. Sew a 12"-long zipper between the lid and the side pieces. Finish sewing the lid and side pieces together (where not attached by the zipper). Decorate with white skull-and-crossbones motifs.

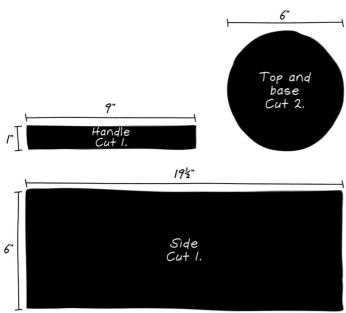

6"

Top and base
Cut 2.

9"

1"

Handle
Cut 1.

19½"

6"

Side
Cut 1.

Desk Pad

Cut a 17¾" x 17¾" piece of heavy poster board. Cut two corner triangles from black felt using the measurements on page 116. Trim the diagonal edge on each triangle with a blanket stitch (see "Blanket Stitch" on page 11). Glue the triangles to the bottom corners the poster board. Cut a 2½" x 17¾" strip of black felt and four white skull-and-crossbones motifs. Glue the skulls securely to the felt strip, and then glue the strip to the top of the poster board.

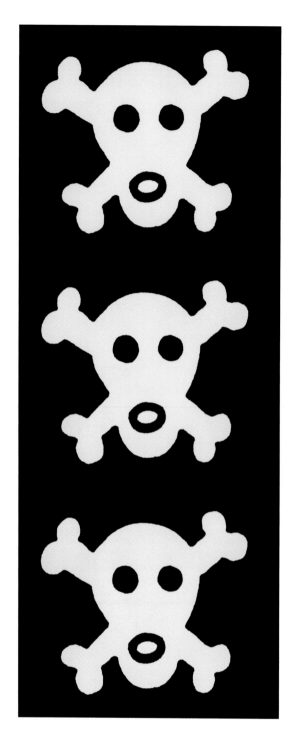

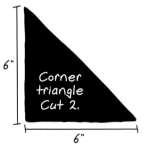

6"

Corner
triangle
Cut 2.

6"

Pencil Cup

You can make a pencil cup using the same method
as for the wastepaper basket on pages 75 and 76. Cut
out a template from heavy plastic or use a glass that
is the right size. Felt the piece on the glass and, when
the felt is dry, decorate it with a skull-and-crossbones
motif as shown.

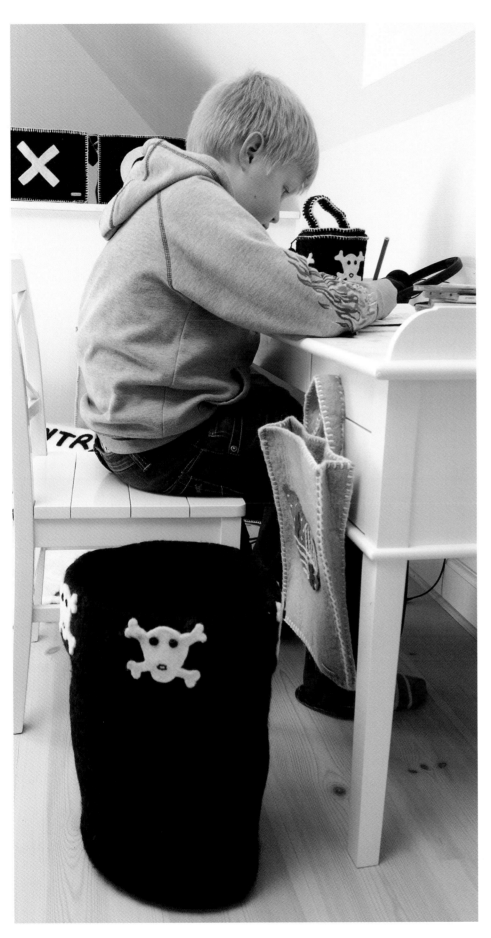

Wastepaper Basket

Make a wastepaper basket using the technique on pages 75 and 76. Fold down the edge and decorate with white skull-and-crossbones motifs as shown.

BOXES

I wonder what treasures are hidden in these cool boxes?

Cool Box

Enlarge the alphabet patterns on pages 94–97 by 125%. Use the patterns and white felt to cut out the letters. Sew or use fabric glue to attach them to the box front. Cut and sew the boxes using the measurements and technique on page 27. For the handles, cut two 1½" x 12" strips; sew the handles as instructed on page 93.

Cross and Circle Boxes

Use the X and O patterns to cut the shapes from white felt. Sew or use fabric glue to attach them to the box front. Cut and sew the boxes in the same manner as the Cool Box.

Box with a Sword

Cut a sword from light blue felt using the pattern below. Embroider or needle felt the red stripes. Sew or use fabric glue to attach the sword to the box front. Cut and sew the box in the same manner as the Box with a Coat of Arms.

Box with a Coat of Arms

Cut out a light blue moon using the pattern opposite and decorate as shown. The white stripes can be embroidered or needle felted. Cut out the red sword and star. Glue them to the moon, and then glue the moon to the box front as shown above. Cut and sew the boxes using the measurements and technique on page 27. For the handles, cut two 1½" x 12" strips; sew the handles as instructed on page 93.

STORAGE POCKETS

Cut out the pieces, referring to the illustration for measurements and number of pieces to cut. Decorate the front using the motifs on pages 122 and 123. Sew the handle securely to the back. Using a blanket stitch (see "Blanket Stitch" on page 11), sew the side pieces between the front and back pieces. Sew the bottom edge as shown in the photos.

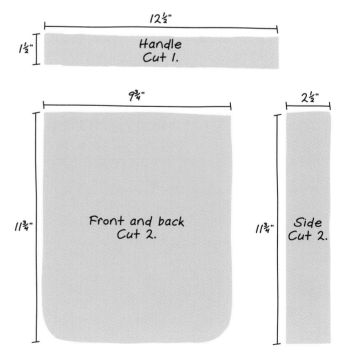

BLACK AND BLUE PILLOWS

Use the patterns on page 121 or the ones on page 126 to cut out the motifs. Sew or use fabric glue to securely attach them to the pillow front. Cut and sew the square pillows using the measurements and instructions on page 33. You may want to add a crocheted edging (see "Crocheted Edging" on page 11).

The white rectangular pillow is made using the measurements on page 91. Enlarge the patterns on pages 94–97 by 125%. Use the patterns and black felt to cut out the letters.

RESOURCES

Batts, Fibers, and Supplies for Wet Felting

Outback Fibers
Georgetown, Texas
www.outbackfibers.com
800-276-5015

New England Felting Supply
Easthampton, Massachusetts
www.feltingsupply.com
413-527-1188

Spritely Goods
Phoenix, Arizona
www.spritelygoods.com

Ready-Made Felt

Weir Dolls and Crafts
Ann Arbor, Michigan
www.weirdollsandcrafts.com
734-668-6992

Woolylady
Eagle River, Wisconsin
www.woolylady.com
715-477-0036

Joggles
West Warwick, Rhode Island
www.joggles.com
401-615-7696

New and Best-Selling Titles from

That Patchwork Place®

America's Best-Loved
Quilt Books®

Martingale® & COMPANY

America's Best-Loved Craft & Hobby Books®
America's Best-Loved Knitting Books®

APPLIQUÉ
Appliqué Quilt Revival
Beautiful Blooms
Cutting-Garden Quilts
Dream Landscapes
Easy Appliqué Blocks
Simple Comforts
Sunbonnet Sue and Scottie Too

BABIES AND CHILDREN
Baby's First Quilts
Let's Pretend
Snuggle-and-Learn Quilts for Kids
Sweet and Simple Baby Quilts
Warm Welcome—NEW!

BEGINNER
Color for the Terrified Quilter
Four-Patch Frolic—NEW!
Happy Endings, Revised Edition
Machine Appliqué for the Terrified Quilter
Quilting Your Style—NEW!
Your First Quilt Book (or it should be!)

GENERAL QUILTMAKING
American Jane's Quilts for All Seasons
Bits and Pieces
Bold and Beautiful
Country-Fresh Quilts
Creating Your Perfect Quilting Space
Fat-Quarter Quilting—NEW!
Fig Tree Quilts: Fresh Vintage Sewing
Folk-Art Favorites
Follow-the-Line Quilting Designs
    Volume Three
Gathered from the Garden
The New Handmade
Points of View
Prairie Children and Their Quilts
Quilt Challenge—NEW!
Quilt Revival
A Quilter's Diary
Quilter's Happy Hour

Quilting for Joy
Quilts from Paradise—NEW!
Remembering Adelia
Simple Seasons
Skinny Quilts and Table Runners
Twice Quilted

HOLIDAY AND SEASONAL
Candy Cane Lane—NEW!
Christmas Quilts from Hopscotch
Comfort and Joy
Deck the Halls—NEW!
Holiday Wrappings

HOOKED RUGS, NEEDLE FELTING, AND PUNCHNEEDLE
Miniature Punchneedle Embroidery
Needle Felting with Cotton and Wool
Needle-Felting Magic

PAPER PIECING
A Year of Paper Piecing
Easy Reversible Vests, Revised Edition
Paper-Pieced Mini Quilts
Show Me How to Paper Piece

PIECING
501 Rotary-Cut Quilt Blocks
Favorite Traditional Quilts Made Easy
Loose Change
Mosaic Picture Quilts
New Cuts for New Quilts
On-Point Quilts
Ribbon Star Quilts
Rolling Along

QUICK QUILTS
40 Fabulous Quick-Cut Quilts
Charmed, I'm Sure—NEW!
Instant Bargello
Quilts on the Double
Sew Fun, Sew Colorful Quilts
Supersize 'Em!

SCRAP QUILTS
Nickel Quilts
Save the Scraps
Scrap-Basket Surprises
Simple Strategies for Scrap Quilts

CRAFTS
A to Z of Sewing
Art from the Heart
The Beader's Handbook
Dolly Mama Beads
Embellished Memories
Friendship Bracelets All Grown Up
Making Beautiful Jewelry
Paper It!
Trading Card Treasures

KNITTING & CROCHET
365 Crochet Stitches a Year
365 Knitting Stitches a Year
A to Z of Knitting
All about Crochet—NEW!
All about Knitting
Amigurumi World
Amigurumi Two!—NEW!
Beyond Wool
Cable Confidence
Casual, Elegant Knits
Crocheted Pursenalities
Knitted Finger Puppets
The Knitter's Book of Finishing
    Techniques
Knitting Circles around Socks
*Knitting More Circles around
    Socks—NEW!*
Knits from the North Sea—NEW!
More Sensational Knitted Socks
*New Twists on Twined Knitting—
    NEW!*
Pursenalities
Simple Stitches
Toe-Up Techniques for Hand-
    Knit Socks, Revised Edition
Together or Separate

Our books are available at bookstores and your favorite craft, fabric, and yarn retailers. If you don't see the title you're looking for, visit us at **www.martingale-pub.com** or contact us at:

1-800-426-3126

International: 1-425-483-3313
Fax: 1-425-486-7596 • Email: info@martingale-pub.com